MAX

TOYS

EVIL CAT

A Fluffy Kitty Gets Mean

elia anie

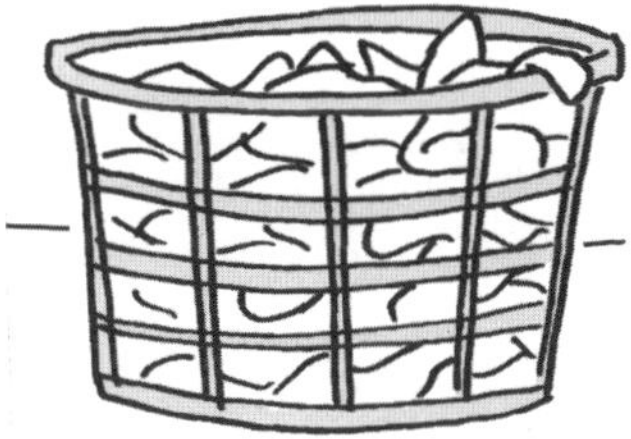

A PERIGEE BOOK

A PERIGEE BOOK
Published by the Penguin Group
Penguin Group (USA) Inc.
375 Hudson Street, New York, New York 10014, USA
Penguin Group (Canada), 90 Eglinton Avenue East, Suite 700, Toronto, Ontario M4P 2Y3, Canada
(a division of Pearson Penguin Canada Inc.)
Penguin Books Ltd., 80 Strand, London WC2R 0RL, England
Penguin Group Ireland, 25 St. Stephen's Green, Dublin 2, Ireland (a division of Penguin Books Ltd.)
Penguin Group (Australia), 250 Camberwell Road, Camberwell, Victoria 3124, Australia
(a division of Pearson Australia Group Pty. Ltd.)
Penguin Books India Pvt. Ltd., 11 Community Centre, Panchsheel Park, New Delhi—110 017, India
Penguin Group (NZ), 67 Apollo Drive, Rosedale, North Shore 0632, New Zealand
(a division of Pearson New Zealand Ltd.)
Penguin Books (South Africa) (Pty.) Ltd., 24 Sturdee Avenue, Rosebank, Johannesburg 2196, South Africa
Penguin Books Ltd., Registered Offices: 80 Strand, London WC2R 0RL, England

EVIL CAT

First American edition: June 2011
Originally published as *Evil Cats* in Great Britain by Headline Publishing Group in 2009.

Perigee trade paperback ISBN: 978-0-399-53673-1

PRINTED IN THE UNITED STATES OF AMERICA

10 9 8 7 6 5 4 3 2 1

SOY SAUCE
WASABI

BUG ZAPPER

TELEMARKETING
DO NOT CALL LIST

GALILEO AND GRAVITY

RoBo-VAC
Vacuum
cleaner

PREMIUM
CRACKERS
CHICKEN SOUP
FOR THE
NINE SOULS

BIRTHDAY
?
WELCOME

HATS
CIVIL WAR REENACTMENT UNIFORMS
UNIFORMS
CIVIL WAR HATS
BLANKS
BLANKS
BLANKS
BLANKS
LIVE AMMO
LIVE AMMO
LIVE AMMO
LIVE AMMO

Mama Mia!

ЧОРНОБИЛЬ
CHERNOBYL

BEANS
BEANS
BEANS
EANS
BEAN
BEANS
EANS
BEAN

BOOM!
LIVES
BEANS

GODZIL
COST
SUSHI MENU

WELCOME
TOYS

CHOCOLATE BUNNY
CHOCOLATE BUNNY
SALE
AHHHHHHH!

FLUFF
FLUFF
FLUFF
FLUFF
FLUFF
FLUFF
FLUFF
FLUFF

WELL, SPEAK UP!
TONGUE

MATH
MATH
MATH
MAX

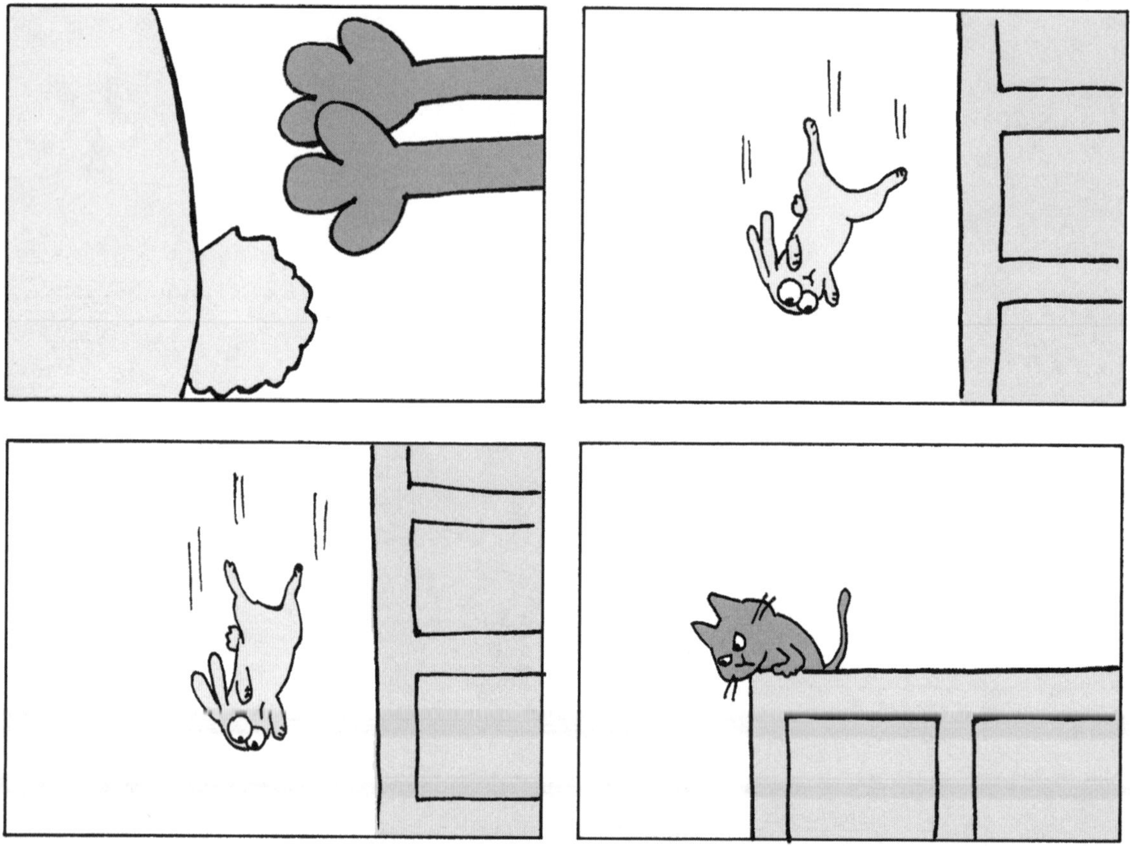

ANIMALS THAT LAND ON THEIR FEET WHEN DROPPED FROM GREAT HEIGHT
CAT ✓
DOG X
RABBIT X
PIG
COW
MOOSE
ELEFANT
GOLDFISH
PORCUPINE

INTERROGATI
HANDBOOK

CONDOMS

100
100
100

DRUG REHAB
Refreshing Coke!

FORTUNE READING

YOU ARE HERE
DIRECTORY
YOU ARE HERE
Penney's
101
102
103
104
121
122
123
124
141
142
143
Kid's Korner
Marshall Jones
131
132
133
151
152
153
154
155
161
162
163
164
165
171
172
173
Macie's

CUCKOO!
CUCKOO
3:05

GENETICALLY
MODIFIED
PLANT FOOD
CARROTS

MARKER

E= ?
E= ?
E= ?
$E=mc^2$
$E=mc^2$

DOG SHOW
142
VIAGRA
DOG TREAT

CRIME SCENE
CHRONICLES
DO
DO NOT CROSS
DO NOT CROSS

MAIL
MAIL

LABEL MAKER
WILLY WONKA AND THE
VEGETABLE FACTORY
2:00 PM SUNDAY

FOR SANTA
CHIPS

OFF
ON
12:00

Exercises to develop OPPOSABLE THUMB
EVOLUTION
DARWIN FOR CATS

SYMPTOMS OF RABIES
WHIPP
CREAM

101 USES FOR A DEAD HUMAN
CAT

LICE

Tyde
JO

-LAX

One fish

two fish

red fish

dead fish

MENU
ck Burger
Rolls
eat Pies
DESSERT
akes & Pudding
Ice Cream
MENU
egemite Burger
e Rolls
OPEN
OUTBACK CAFE
NEXT TOWN
4,000 km
MENU
Vegemite Burger
Vegemite Rolls
Vegemite Pies
DESSERT
egemite Pudding
gemite Ice Cream
KANGAROO SOUVENIRS
U.S.A.

A·B·C
CHALKBOARD

FLOSS
FLOSS
FLOSS
FLOSS
FLOSS

2

THE FIVE HORSEMEN OF THE APOCALYPSE:
WAR, FAMINE, PESTILENCE, DEATH... AND VERY BAD ALLERGIES.

PEPPER
ACHOOO!

Recycle
BOTTLES ONLY
Recycle
CANS ONLY

CAUTION
DINGOS

EUREKA!
ARCHIMEDES c. 287 BC - c. 212 BC

..4..5..6
..7..8..9..10
8
10 ITEMS OR LESS

MARKING YOUR TERRITORY

WHITE OUT
WHERE'S WALDO?

HENRY VIII 1536

HONEY, WHERE'S THE #@$?% REMOTE?!?

SOX
SOCKS

YAK
YAK
YAK
YAK
YAK
CLICK
CLICK
CLICK
FriendSpace.com
CLOSE
YOU HAVE
Ø FRIENDS

VOODOO BOOK
GLUE

NATIONAL BANK
BANK BAILOUT FUNDS
BANK BAILOUT FUNDS

This cat will steal your heart. Literally.
k all cats are sweet
can melt even the hardest of hearts? Think again.
5 hilarious cartoons, Elia Anie shows all the reprehensible
hs to which one particularly malevolent feline can sink.
When she is not fleeing from all things feline,
Elia Anie likes to ponder on things of consequence.
She currently lives in a giant litter box.
EVIL CAT
EVIL CAT
A Fluffy Kitty
Gets Mean